T0024037

365 DAYS OF

calm

DAILY GUIDANCE FOR
INNER PEACE

Robyn Martin

An Hachette UK Company
www.hachette.co.uk

Vie Books, an imprint of Summersdale Publishers Ltd
Part of Octopus Publishing Group Limited
Carmelite House
50 Victoria Embankment
LONDON
EC4Y 0DZ
UK

www.summersdale.com

Printed and bound in China

ISBN: 978-1-80007-443-9

Substantial discounts on bulk quantities of Summersdale books are available to corporations, professional associations and other organizations. For details contact general enquiries: telephone: +44 (0) 1243 771107 or email: enquiries@summersdale.com.

To ....

From ....

introduction

We live in a world that challenges our sense of calm and tranquillity every day. Slipping into anxiety and stress often feels a lot easier than finding calmness and keeping a cool head. Simply put, we're bombarded by things that will inevitably pull us away from even the strongest, hardest-earned feelings of calm.

That being said, there is also hope for each of us to continually reach out for the peace and calm we deserve, for our bodies and minds. As many ways as there are for life to bring stress and worry into the equation, there are equally ways for us to creatively pull back into a place of calm and tranquil energy.

This book is loaded with calming strategies and relaxing tips – one for each day of the year, in fact – and it's here to be a partner and guide for the moments in life that prove overwhelming, when your own calm-down strategies aren't quite working how you'd like. Whether you use it day by day, or flip around, picking out suggestions that resonate with you at the moment, trying any of these methods and incorporating these tactics into your daily life is a sure-fire way to recentre, soothe your mind, and ease your body, bit by bit, until calm is much easier to achieve.

january

As you enter the new year, make a list of the biggest blessings you have in your life, even if they might seem small to others. Read through the list anytime you need a reminder of the wonderful joys you have all around you.

When you wake this morning, take a moment to sit in bed, be still and breathe deeply before getting up and being active. It always helps to start any day with a few minutes of calm and tranquillity.

03

The world may feel like it's spinning out of control, but you don't have to.

HANIA KHURI-TRAPPER

04

Slowly stretch your arms out to the side and then up and over the top of your head. Reach up to the sky, stretching as much as you can toward the sun. Hold that position for a minute, or repeat the movement until you feel a bit more relaxed.

●●● (**05**) ●●●

Brew a cup of tea, in the most calming way you can. Take the time to set a kettle to boil, and watch for the steam to rise. Select your favourite herbal tea leaves or bag and prepare a full teapot for yourself. Enjoy sipping this soothing infusion while you sit in your favourite spot.

●●● (**06**) ●●●

Indulge in comfort. Throw on the fuzzy socks and sweatshirt that make you happy and wrap up in the cosiest blanket you have.

●●● (**07**) ●●●

If you feel stressed, grab a pad of paper and doodle freely. Putting down swirls and scribbles and jagged lines can help to ease your mind.

Listen to your favourite song this morning. Or a few favourite songs. Or put them on repeat and groove through the morning.

Take a moment out of your day and write a letter to your favourite person in the world. It may feel a bit outdated, but you might also find that stepping away from screens to write about your life or tell stories to a loved one on paper can be so much more peaceful – and they'll love the sentiment.

Drink a glass of juice. If possible, take the time to squeeze it fresh, even if it takes a bit longer. The act can be cathartic, and the juice itself is a mood and energy boost.

In overwhelming moments, pause, close your eyes and focus your attention on your feet and the ground below you. Actively "push" down, feeling your connection to the earth and focusing on grounding yourself until you feel calmer.

If you change your mind, you can change your life.

MICHELLE WILLIAMS

If you have a fireplace or outdoor pit, start a fire and enjoy the calm energy provided by looking at the moving flames and listening to the crackle. If you don't have either, the same thing applies to lighting a candle and watching the flickering flame as the wick burns down.

You have to be strong and calm
to overcome difficult moments.

DANI ALVES

●●● (15) ●●●

Get outside and walk for 30 minutes or as long as you can. Choose an area in nature or with some greenery if possible, as this is also shown to increase your calmness.

●●● (16) ●●●

Take a day off from drinking coffee and see if you feel less anxious. Swap it with a cup of herbal tea or a glass of water or juice. If you need at least a bit of caffeine, even some black tea is a better option.

Take a huge breath in and hold it for a count of four. Exhale slowly. This alone does a quick mental reset.

Spend a few moments reading some poetry. Offering words of wisdom and a bit of respite from the daily grind, poems are a quick and simple way to start the day. Emily Dickinson, Maya Angelou, Walt Whitman and Rupi Kaur are a few well-loved poets with uplifting, calming messages.

19

Nothing can cure the soul but the senses, just as nothing can cure the senses but the soul.

OSCAR WILDE

Take a look at your desk, or any space where you do work. Gather up all the items needing your attention – the old mail, incomplete paperwork, or even scraps of rubbish and clutter. Throw away what you don't need, and take time to finish the tasks you've been putting off. Crossing off a few of these things from your mental stress-list brings a great feeling of relief.

••• 21 •••

Peel an orange, or another citrus fruit. This simple, intentional act provides a great moment of mental focus. Then, of course, enjoy eating the orange too.

••• 22 •••

Do a bit of landscaping. Trim the grass, pull some weeds, prune a bush, water some vegetables, or whatever suits you. Just get outside and work with your hands. If you don't have a garden, find a friend's to help out in.

••• 23 •••

Talk positively to yourself. Throughout the day, give yourself compliments and encouraging feedback, whether things are going well or not. Acknowledge something you love about yourself.

Take care of your skin. Use a face mask while you rest for the evening. Then do a full skincare routine, gently cleansing your face, exfoliating and moisturizing. Use all the best-smelling products you have.

You should feel beautiful and you should feel safe. What you surround yourself with should bring you peace of mind and peace of spirit.

STACY LONDON

Although it may not seem enjoyable, studies have shown that a cold shower could be beneficial to ease anxiety, lower blood pressure, increase endorphins and decrease inflammation. But if you aren't ready for a full soak, holding an ice cube in your hand or rubbing it across your arms, placing an ice pack on the back of your neck, or freezing a damp towel and patting it on your face all have a similar cool-to-calm effect.

Select a comfortable spot on the floor and curl up into child's pose: buttocks lowered to heels, forehead to the earth and arms by your side. Hold this position, stretching and releasing tension, for at least a few minutes or until your body feels looser and your breathing calmer.

28

When we are unable to find
tranquillity within ourselves,
it is useless to seek it elsewhere.

FRANÇOIS DE LA ROCHEFOUCAULD

Cut out some small slips of paper and write, on
each one, something that is frustrating you or
worrying you today. Don't hold back on these
concerns, big or small. Then, one by one, physically
destroy these papers, whether by tossing them in
a fireplace, shredding them and recycling them,
or finding an even more creative way of (safely)
ridding yourself of them.

• • • (30) • • •

Find a fairly comfortable but firm area on the floor. Place a pillow under your head or knees if needed, and lie flat on the firm surface, focusing on the feeling of your body touching the ground. Count to 300 (or more, if you prefer!) before getting up and carrying on with your day.

• • • (31) • • •

Start the day with an honest self-conversation. Ask yourself: "What's on my mind or causing anxiety?" Then reflect on any possible ways to conquer that situation or feeling so it no longer burdens you. Finish by repeating to yourself: "I can let go of anxious feelings. This situation is temporary."

february

Walk through your home, or even just one room, and look critically at your belongings. Which ones no longer serve a purpose or create positive feelings? Give yourself permission to get rid of four or five items, and then do so, donating them or gifting them to others who might derive joy from them.

Sip on a cup of calming lavender or mint tea before bed, and enjoy an activity that is technology-free. Read a book, do a crossword puzzle, play a game, or do a bit of knitting.

It's time to clear out your email inbox. While the idea of commencing this task is unlikely to inspire calm, the feeling at the end when you see that number reduced down from hundreds (or thousands!) is so worth it.

··●(04)●··

Enjoy an evening of your favourite self-care. There is no one right way, and everyone finds self-care in different practices, so personalize the evening. Perhaps you like to read all night in your comfiest pajamas. Perhaps it's playing a card game or doing crosswords or taking a long bath or logging on to a favourite video game or going for a run. Prioritize one of these things tonight.

Find a way to spend time with animals. If you have your own pets, this should be easy. Snuggle up with your dog or cat for a bit. Even if you have a less cuddly creature, watching them roam or swim about their home can be soothing. If you don't have a pet of your own, hang out with a friend or relative who does, or even just swing by an animal shelter to pet some dogs (they'll appreciate it too!).

Light a candle this evening and let its delicate flame bring you a sense of serenity.

••• (07) •••

If you find yourself feeling stressed over something, ask yourself if, in the grand scheme of things, the stress is worth it. By letting go of negative energy you'll boost your sense of well-being.

••• (08) •••

Start or end the day with a refreshing cold shower. The thought may make you shudder, but the cold provides a mental reset, and slipping into warm clothes afterward will cement that calm feeling.

••• (09) •••

Put blue in your field of vision. Based on colour psychology, blue conjures more feelings of calmness and serenity, so looking at the blue sky, wearing blue, or changing your computer desktop to a nice image of blue water could all boost your peaceful feelings.

10

Set your heart on doing good. Do it over and over again and you will be filled with joy.

BUDDHA

Put on your favourite song, turn up the volume and sing along, with as much enthusiasm as you can muster. Release as much negative energy and worry as you can through your body in those few minutes. And if you need to, repeat the song once or twice until you really feel reset.

• • • • • •

Consciously question your anxious thoughts. When something arises, observe the anxiety and ask yourself, "Is this worth worrying about right now? What do I gain by giving in to this anxiety?" Try to observe the feeling from a logical perspective until you can determine which thoughts are able to be set aside.

• • • (13) • • •

Go for a long walk or hike. If you can find somewhere removed from normal life and surrounded by natural beauty, all the better. Push yourself to go longer than you normally would for an extra head-clearing effect.

••• •••

Eat a snack that comes in small individual pieces. Perhaps it's a bowl of pretzels, grapes or nuts. Eat one single item at a time, drawing out the process and focusing on the food you're eating.

••• 15 •••

When you need to calm down today, try reciting one or a few of these mantras:

- I deserve to savour peaceful moments today.
- I give myself permission to protect my own energy.
- I have the power to step back and remain calm.
- I choose to dedicate my mind to thoughts that feel good.
- I can hit refresh anytime I need to.

Head to the shops and buy yourself a bouquet of flowers to put on your table. Or, if the option is available, head out into your own garden and collect a bouquet from your own plants.

••• (17) •••

Go to any music streaming platform, run a quick search for "relaxing music" and select a nice playlist to pop on as you get ready, drive to work, take care of chores or do anything else that makes you feel less than peaceful.

••• (18) •••

Try to take a short bike ride today, particularly at a time when you're in need of a change of scenery.

Try this exercise to relieve stress in the body. Starting at your feet, fully tense your muscles, hold for a moment, then relax them entirely. Do this muscle group by muscle group up your entire body until you reach your head.

Wrap a soft blanket around your shoulders, sit somewhere comfortable and grab a large pillow. Squeeze the pillow to your body with all your effort, intentionally releasing tension into the movement. After a few moments, you should feel more calm, but this is a technique you can return to anytime.

The question isn't if we can weather this unknown,

But how we will weather this unknown together.

AMANDA GORMAN

Say no when you need to. If you feel yourself teetering on the edge of crisis, anger or panic, choose to say no to things when you're able to. If you're asked whether you can take on more at work, the answer can sometimes be a polite "no". Or what about when you're asked whether you can run some extra errands or if you want to get together with friends at the last minute? When you need to say no, you can. You deserve time for yourself too.

••• (23) •••

Try some calming, anxiety-reducing foods. Studies have shown pumpkin seeds, dark chocolate, eggs, chamomile (try a nice cup of tea), almonds and Brazil nuts to be among foods that can reduce anxiety levels over time.

••• (24) •••

Take a news break. If you're a morning news watcher, skip it for the day and try watching something comical instead. If you tend to scroll through online news updates or listen to news radio, take a day off and see if you feel any calmer stepping away from it for a bit.

••• (25) •••

Choose a favourite musical artist or group that always makes you feel good. Press play on one of their albums and listen to it all the way through, even as you do other things and go about your day.

••• (26) •••

Drink an entire glass of water in the morning, before doing much else. Anytime you feel your tension rising throughout the day, pause, drink at least half a glass of water, and get back to it. Sometimes dehydration can have a quiet, but surprising effect on us.

••• (27) •••

Suck on a mint during the day, whenever you need to cool and calm down any racing thoughts.

••• •••

Go through old photos and pick one from a moment when you were totally happy and at peace. Set it as your phone's lock screen, at least for the day, or for as long as you'd like, so you see it each time you check your phone.

••• (29) •••

Get online and search for yoga videos. Follow along with an instruction video that matches your skills and schedule. Whether you have a few minutes to do a bit of stretching, or you can commit to a refreshing hour-long class, the movements should soothe you.

march

Cook yourself a vibrant, nourishing meal today, loaded with ingredients that you love and that your body loves. Take your time with the steps, relaxing into the calming rhythm of tasks like chopping vegetables.

Start a journal, or write in one you already have. Make a point of noting the things in your day that caused negative feelings to arise, and the things that brought you back to a place of calm.

••• •••

Delegate when you can. Rather than letting your plate pile up with commitments and requests and excess work, find opportunities to pass along tasks to others in your life, and watch as your mind relaxes. You'll find you have more people in your life to delegate to than you might realize.

••• (04) •••

If the day has you overwhelmed, spend the night cosy and comfortable in bed or on the couch. Grab a delicious snack. Stay hydrated. Then pop on a favourite childhood movie and feel the cares melt away.

Find someone to give you a long, comforting hug. Loving hugs can be absolute magic for the nervous system.

Start a "calm down" playlist on any music-streaming platform you use. Whenever you hear a song that makes you feel calm, relaxed and happy, add it to the list. After a bit you'll have a go-to mix to pop on anytime you need to de-stress.

••• 07 •••

Try lifting some weights. That can mean many things to many people, so just do what works for you. Whether it's lifting some small weights while you listen to music or doing a huge set of high-weight exercises, you'll focus on your body rather than wandering thoughts, ending up with a calmer feeling (and plenty of endorphins) afterward.

Admit your feelings to yourself. If you're feeling anxious or angry or burnt out, don't pretend to yourself that you're just fine. That's not doing you any favours. You can only start to ease away from those feelings and into tranquillity if you accept how you're really feeling first.

Laughter keeps everyone feeling wonderful.

BETTY WHITE

Take a page from the queen of positivity herself and use laughter to ease your mind. Whatever makes you laugh — whether it's a stand-up special, a beloved sitcom, a best friend or some YouTube videos — this is what you should make time for today.

11

Humans make perhaps as many as 35,000 decisions per day, vastly more than we ever realize. But if there are choices in your life you're waiting to make, they're likely weighing on you and keeping you from feeling calm. Choose one decision to be made, whether it's small or large, and commit to it. Let yourself be freed from a little weight.

12

If we do each thing calmly and carefully we will get it done quicker and with much less stress.

VIGGO MORTENSEN

Let in the light! Don't keep your blinds or curtains shut all day. Open them up and let the natural light shine in and brighten your room and mental space.

Find any untidy cabinet or drawer in your home and take a few minutes to clean it up and reorganize it. Throw out any rubbish or things you don't need and get this one small place to a state you're happy with.

Put up wind chimes or a rain chain near your home and enjoy the sweet, melodic sounds bringing you calming energy throughout the day.

• • • (16) • • •

Take a meditative, resetting walk. No matter the mindset you start in, focus on mindfulness and clearing out anxious thoughts one by one as you go. Tune your attention into the sound of the breeze or people passing by. Focus on the singular feeling of your feet making contact with the ground again and again.

• • • (17) • • •

Reduce irritating and unnecessary noises in your space. Turn the phone ringer off, close the window if there's drilling outside, turn off any screens that aren't being watched. Create quieter spaces for calmer thoughts to flourish.

Move your body. (Preferably a bit chaotically.) If you can, stand up with plenty of space around you and wildly swing your arms and legs from side to side, back and forth, in circles, and so on. No matter how it looks, moving with abandon will help shake out all your worries.

Quiet is peace. Tranquillity.
Quiet is turning down the
volume knob on life.

KHALED HOSSEINI

•••(20)•••

Find somewhere safe and comfortable to stand, then balance on one foot, focusing your energy and thoughts on your body. After a minute or two, switch to the other foot.

•••(21)•••

Whether you have many already, or none at all, buy a small plant for your home. Put it on a windowsill or on your desk, pay attention to its care, and reflect on the happy feelings brought about by having a little living greenery in your space.

•••(22)•••

Declutter your phone. Clear out the old voicemails. Delete or respond to the lingering texts. Get rid of the apps taking up space. Save your old photos.

•••(23)•••

Rather than waking up and immediately rushing into intense action, start the morning with a cup of water, followed by a cup of herbal tea and a few moments of reflective contemplation on the day ahead.

•••(24)•••

If an invite to do something makes you feel more overwhelmed than excited, choose to pass on it this time around.

••• (25) •••

We are always getting ready
to live but never living.

RALPH WALDO EMERSON

Sit somewhere comfortable and stretch one leg out
to the side, with your other leg tucked in. Stretch
your fingers out to reach for the extended foot and
hold that position. Switch which leg is extended
and do the same on the other side.

Try to ditch the wake-up alarm, or at least get it down to one instead of a series. Each time that beeping returns, your calm feelings are replaced by tension. If possible, train yourself to wake up naturally, or with the morning light. If you can't, at least try a more peaceful sound effect for the alarm you use.

••• (28) •••

Spend some time knitting. If you don't already know how, it's a great, mind-soothing activity that can help you unwind at the end of the day, and there are tons of tutorials online.

••• (29) •••

Grab a stress ball. They really do work wonders.

Peace cannot be kept by
force. It can only be achieved
by understanding.

ALBERT EINSTEIN

Breathe in through your nose and out through
your mouth. Focus your attention to these slow,
rhythmic breaths, not concerning yourself with
anything besides your beautiful ability to continue
breathing in and out.

april

Focus on the present and the future. Lingering on thoughts of the past or "should-have-beens" brings no peace. Keeping your attention on the current moment allows you to be more present and mindful. And finding things to look forward to and be excited about in the future can relieve some anxiety around the unknowns that are also ahead.

Wash your hair. And not just like you would during any normal shower. Put a little extra time and love into it. Scrub and massage the shampoo into your scalp, enjoy standing in the hot water and then, after rinsing, repeat the shampooing process. Indulge in some salon-quality hair-washing from your own hands.

••• (03) •••

Don't judge each day by the harvest you reap but by the seeds that you plant.

ROBERT LOUIS STEVENSON

Take the time to walk around your home and water every plant. Trim off dead leaves or give them a turn to face the sun. Take care with the process and make sure each plant, whether you have three or fifty, gets some love.

••• (05) •••

Grab a colouring book (whether it's meant for adults or not), some colouring supplies, and get into it. You can put on some TV or music as you do, or focus entirely on just putting colour on the page, whichever provides a more relaxing environment.

Think about a grudge or resentment you're holding onto. Ask yourself: "Is this negative feeling bringing me any relief? Is being bitter or resentful helping me improve my life?" If not, work on letting go of that feeling, choosing forgiveness or even just acceptance, and letting the part of your mind that held those feelings finally calm down.

Call a grandparent, an elderly friend or neighbour – really anyone who you see as a mentor, or wise figure in your life. Talk to them about anything, but try asking one of these questions:

- Do you wish you'd spent less of your life worrying?

- What are your strongest memories of your life?

••• (08) •••

You don't get to choose how you're going to die, or when. You can only decide how you're going to live now.

JOAN BAEZ

••• (09) •••

Worry less about what people think of you. Yes, easier said than done. But making a conscious decision to put less stock in what others may or may not be thinking about you can lead to a truly soothing outcome.

••• (10) •••

Indulge in some mindless TV. Anything that doesn't require a lot of thought or attention on your end and offers a little bit of end-of-the-day wind-down time is a great choice, even if it feels like a "guilty pleasure".

Head outside and find a tree that calls to you. Bring a blanket or cushion if needed, and set yourself up sitting beneath the tree, against the trunk if possible. Gaze up at the leaves and branches, take some deep breaths, and let its presence ground you.

Start recording your dreams, anything you can remember, when you wake up each day. Use this time as a transition from sleeping to waking, and as a chance to explore some of the things that may be on your mind and presenting themselves in your sleep.

••• 13 •••

Stretch your arms high above your head, wide out to your sides, and far down to your feet, moving slowly and smoothly between each position.

14

Each person deserves a day
away in which no problems
are confronted, no solutions
searched for. Each of us needs to
withdraw from the cares which
will not withdraw from us.

MAYA ANGELOU

15

Put on some lotion, taking the time and care
to moisturize your hands, arms, feet, legs and
anywhere else that could use it. If you have a lotion
with a soothing scent like lavender, all the better.

Sleep in, even just a bit. Choose a day when you're not working or don't have morning meetings, so the extra sleep lets you wake up refreshed, not more stressed.

Make a "calm me" collage. Grab some old magazines, photos or anything else you have on hand. Flip through and collect any images that soothe your mind, whether it's tropical scenes, water, satisfying patterns, beautifully decorated rooms or anything else. Glue them to a large sheet of paper that you can set up near your desk and gaze at anytime you need a calming backdrop.

●●● 18 ●●●

If the day is cold, relax in the evening with a hot chocolate. And add the marshmallows – they're important.

Try an ultra-simple solo sound bath. In a quiet, empty room, get comfortable and either use a pre-recorded sound bath video (there are some online), or use chimes, a singing bowl, tuning forks or the like to fill the space with cleansing, calming sound. Experiment to see what works best for you.

••● **20** ●••

Put on healing lip balm. Taking care of even tiny parts of your body can have a surprising effect on the way you feel as a whole. And chapped lips are never going to help you calm down.

When anxious thoughts arise, pause and ask: "Is this the most pressing issue in my day?" See if you can use this grounding question to remember that many anxious thoughts needn't be more than fleeting.

••• (22) •••

Do something you enjoy that requires intense focus, something that doesn't allow for multitasking or even thinking about any other things while you do it. Playing an instrument is a perfect example, as is reading a book or cooking a complex meal.

••• (23) •••

Bend over at the waist so your head is below your torso. Hold this position for a minute, letting yourself reset.

Pull out a favourite book from your childhood and spend a cosy afternoon escaping into whatever world you loved when you were young.

Update your planner. Make sure you're caught up to the current week, then spend a bit of time looking ahead and making a note of plans, events, appointments and birthdays. This should help ease worries that there's some plan you're forgetting about.

••● 26 ●••

Rainy days should be spent at home with a cup of tea and a good book.

BILL WATTERSON

Snack on a bit of dark chocolate. It's good for the mood and brain, without giving too much of an unhelpful sugar boost and crash.

Chew on some gum, especially during a commute, while on hold on the phone, or at any other time when those stress levels might be peaking. The repetitive motion provides a welcome distraction and can even improve your mood too.

Head to a bookshelf and riffle through a few books. Choose books you love, or ones that are heavy in images and art. Spend some time admiring the photos or reading bits and pieces, and enjoy successfully distracting yourself for at least a short while.

Write a list of feelings you experience throughout the day, trying not to filter any out. Use this log to see the range of emotions you go through every day, which is healthy and normal, and to push those feelings externally onto the page (this can help a lot).

may

Treat yourself to a massage this month. If it's out of the budget, find a partner or loved one willing to give you a little back, neck or foot massage when you're in real need of some relaxation.

Eat a little more honey. The natural sweetener has lots of health benefits, including helping to reduce anxiety. Drizzle a bit of honey in tea or coffee, on your dessert or on some toast.

● ● ● ● ● ●

Make a positivity list. End the day by writing out a list of all the things you felt happy about or grateful for throughout the day.

● ● ● ● ● ●

Picture your happy place. It's a bit of a clichéd concept now, but the core of it actually works wonders. Create a happy place you can visualize in great detail. It should be either a place you know and find deep comfort in, or an imagined space that calms you down. Picture it in crisp detail, from the smells and the feelings on your skin to the sounds around you. Close your eyes and drift to this place for a moment when you need to.

Pop on some nature sounds. (You can find them on YouTube or any music streaming platform.) Whether it's rain, waves, rainforest or something else, the ambient noise is shown to have a calming, almost meditative effect.

••• (06) •••

If warm tea or coffee isn't for you, especially if the caffeine will keep you awake, try sipping warm milk before heading to bed.

••• (07) •••

Use a foot soak, mask or scrub to indulge in a little relaxing self-care and get your feet feeling luxurious and soft.

●●● ●●●

Grab a pillow and yell into it, at the top of your lungs. The old movie cliché for relieving tension and calming down may seem silly, but it works miraculously well for letting a lot of the negative energy out and leaving you feeling more zen.

●●● ●●●

Pick up a light therapy lamp and set it up on your desk or bedside table where it'll be on you often. Designed to relieve the symptoms of SAD (seasonal affective disorder), these lamps provide bright, sunlight-mimicking light, meant to boost mood and reduce the effects of seasonal depression and anxiety.

●●●(10)●●●

The beginning of health is sleep.

IRISH PROVERB

●●●(11)●●●

Start today by reminding yourself that this is just one day in a whole wild, wonderful, chaotic life. Tomorrow the sun will rise again, and you'll have a whole new day of opportunities ahead. This day, this one day, is not the end-all be-all of whether you'll have a happy life.

●●●(12)●●●

Find an old phone book or other thick, unimportant book and keep it with you during times of stress. When you need to cool off, start ripping through big stacks of pages at a time, putting all your energy and focus into the task.

13

Almost everything will work
again if you unplug it for a
few minutes, including you.

ANNE LAMOTT

Hit the pool (or lake or river). Get in the water
and do some swimming. Not only is it a full-body
exercise, which boosts endorphins and improves
your mood, but water is also a calming element,
and the feeling of soothing water encircling you is
enough to bring anxiety levels way down for quite
a while.

Pick up a container of modelling clay and keep it on hand to squeeze, mould or squish when tensions are high. It's just about the cheapest calming tool out there, and brings you right back to childhood.

Find a beautiful sunny spot in a park and sit peacefully. Bring a snack if you'd like, but mainly just watch people pass by, letting it be a reminder that you are one small piece of a community and everyone else around you is living a similarly complex, unpredictable yet beautiful life.

Eat some mango! Mangoes share a compound with lavender, the herb known for calming the body and mind. Plus, the act of peeling and slicing a mango requires focus and calms you as well.

••• (18) •••

What hard conversation have you been avoiding having with yourself? Stop putting it off and work through it. You'll feel better.

••• (19) •••

Treat yourself to a long, hot bath. Use Epsom salts or bubble bath. Get your space loaded up with calming tools: candles, peaceful music, low lighting, a book, tea or wine, and extra soft towels and pajamas to get into when you're done. Let it be your ultimate relaxation for the week, and don't feel bad about taking the time.

Make a bubble wrap box or basket. Save all the bubble wrapping that comes in your packages and, rather than throw it out, collect it in a specific spot. When you need to relax, reach your hands in and start popping the tension away. Or pull out a piece to step all over.

Grab a handful of dry rice and let it fall through your fingers. Scoop it up and do this again and again.

If you get tired, learn to rest, not to quit.

BANKSY

Turn to the classics. Find a lava lamp, often sold at affordable prices online. Plug it in, heat it up and watch it turn into a tiny world of calm.

● ● ● (24) ● ● ●

Find a local garden centre and walk aimlessly around it, stroking soft leaves of plants, smelling flowers, and taking in the greenery. And of course, if you can, buy something to bring home.

Do a mini self-massage – on your head. Press and hold your fingers to the centre of your forehead for several seconds. Then move them to your temples and make small circular movements while pressing gently there. Press under your ears and circle your fingers there while applying pressure. Rub your fingers along each side of your nose, across your cheekbone and up around the sides of your eyes.

26

Every one of us needs to show how much we care for each other and, in the process, care for ourselves.

DIANA, PRINCESS OF WALES

••• (27) •••

Eat something crunchy. The combination of the sound, movement, texture and taste does a lot of good for calming spiralling anxiety.

••• (28) •••

Head outside on a warm, lovely evening, have a seat in the grass, and watch for the stars to come out.

••• (29) •••

When you notice yourself tensing or stressing, consciously tune back into your body, assess how it's feeling... and release your tongue from the roof of your mouth.

30

**Stop trying to define who
you are and just be.**

CARA DELEVINGNE

Try submerging yourself in some water. Whether
a bathtub, pool, lake or hot tub, if you can find
enough water, lower yourself in, and submerge
yourself so your head is covered. Don't feel the
need to stay under too long. Pop back up, take a
breath and submerge again if it helps. The act of
gentle submersion is a great brain and body reset.

june

Try out CBD. The natural chemical does not produce any high, and instead interacts with central nervous system receptors, producing a calming effect, and potentially even reducing inflammation or pain. There are CBD products online and in many stores, and you can find it in formats ranging from tinctures and topical balms to edible oils, confectionery and drinks.

••• (02) •••

Recite the alphabet backward. Reminiscent of a juvenile game, dedicating your brain's energy and focus to a task like this allows all the other stresses and overwhelming thoughts to vanish.

••• (03) •••

Spend all day in your softest, cosiest socks or slippers. Even if you're heading out of the house, just pop shoes on over those fuzzy socks and carry on.

••• (04) •••

Do some vigorous exercise. Of course, choose something you like and feel capable of doing. But a long bike ride, hard hike, exercise class, swim, weightlifting session, Pilates or other intensive activity has a powerful effect on your mind as well.

••• (05) •••

Breathe. Let go. And remind yourself that this very moment is the only one you know you have for sure.

OPRAH WINFREY

••• (06) •••

Do some outdoor work. While it doesn't sound appealing most of the time, it should have three positive outcomes. One, it's another great form of intensive, endorphin-boosting exercise. Two, it gets you out in the sun and surrounded by greenery, both proven to improve your mental state. And three, the satisfaction at accomplishing that major, set-aside project will provide an amazing feeling of calm.

Take a few moments to sit down and visualize how you want your life to look, how you want to feel, where you want to be. Picture these things in great detail. There is a lot of manifestation power in this, and it can also be very calming to see more clearly what you want, so you can start to move toward it.

Close your eyes for a while. Not to sleep, but simply to remove the external stimulation that may be keeping you from calm.

Get to a park and hop on a swing. Let yourself feel like a kid again, and remember why that can be a good thing.

Try some Bach flower remedies. A natural healing tool around since the 1930s, these tinctures use floral properties to cast away negative feelings and balance the mind. Elm, Rock Rose, and Rescue Remedy may all be good for calming down.

Do some painting. Whether it's grabbing some watercolours and a notebook, painting your nails or painting an accent wall in your house, the medium is creative, meditative and thoroughly calming.

On a windy or breezy day, sit outside comfortably and simply revel in the wind. Feel the sensation of it on your skin, listen to the sounds it makes whipping through branches, or watch how it makes leaves dance.

Express your gratitude out loud, almost like a prayer. Thank your deity or deities, the universe or your life itself (whichever you prefer) for the small gifts of your day.

Try to stabilize your sleep schedule. Getting to bed and waking up around the same time daily can prove beneficial for stabilizing moods too.

15

Rest and be thankful.

WILLIAM WORDSWORTH

Keep fresh air circulating in your home, whenever possible. If the weather is nice, keep the windows open. Let that fresh, comforting air in, keeping your home's energy much more positive. Plus, you may get the benefits of birdsong or other peaceful accompaniments.

••• (17) •••

Count from one to 100. Then count backward from 100 down to one. If this exercise calms you, do it again whenever required.

••• (18) •••

Head outside and blow bubbles with complete abandon, like your childhood self. Watch them float away or pop them with your fingers.

••• (19) •••

Treat yourself to a hand massage. Put on some luxurious lotion and rub it in slowly and methodically, applying pressure between your fingers and along each one, as well as around the palm, moving in circles and pressing more firmly in spots that feel tense.

Hang a bird feeder outside your window. Preferably choose a window you sit or stand near often, whether it's by your kitchen sink or your desk. Keep it replenished and just watch how much peace and happiness these little visitors can bring.

Find a smooth, flat stone you can use as a worry rock. Anything that is a good shape and size to rub your thumb along in times of stress will work perfectly. Keep it in your pocket to rub subtly when you need a bit of a calming effect.

••• (22) •••

Go for a long run around your neighbourhood, at any pace that suits you.

••• (23) •••

Turn on your favourite music artist and listen to them all morning, while getting ready, eating breakfast or driving.

••• (24) •••

Manage the notifications on your phone. Do the constant popups from apps you never use or group text threads you don't check often cause you stress? Adjust your settings! Let go of the need to see so many constant updates, and focus in on only getting notifications for things that are important.

Make a homemade avocado face mask for a little relaxing self-care. In a food processor, combine:

- 30 g (¼ cup) very ripe avocado
- 2 tbsp raw honey
- ½ tsp apple cider vinegar

Pulse until smooth, spread on your face and enjoy the skin-calming, mind-calming results.

Let your soul stand cool and composed before a million universes.

WALT WHITMAN

Make a personal calm list. Keep track of anything that particularly helps you to feel a little more calm. Even something unexpected that happens to have a noticeable effect on you is perfect. Add these things to a list on your phone so you can turn to it anytime you really need something that'll help.

Whip up a dough! Whether that's a bread dough or another baked good, the acts of measuring out ingredients, mixing things together and seeing your tasty results can be so calming and satisfying. If you are up to the bread challenge, all the better. It's a slow process with lots of peaceful downtime, plus opportunities to knead your stress away.

29

**Knowing how to be solitary
is central to the art of loving.
When we can be alone, we can
be with others without using
them as a means of escape.**

BELL HOOKS

Try acupuncture. If you don't mind the (pain-free) needles, the results of acupuncture sessions can range from pain relief and headache relief to improved sleep and a greater sense of well-being and calm. Seems worth a try!

july

01

If the heat is keeping you from feeling calm, get a bucket of chilled water, add some ice, and set your feet in it for a while.

02

Set out food for squirrels and other furry guests. Squirrels may get a bad reputation as garden pests, but if you learn to embrace them and feed them intentionally, you may find they're actually quite amusing and charming, and can make for hours of peaceful entertainment if you put a feeder near your window.

Fresh air is an instant anxiety reliever so grab your walking gear and head outside for the hills, coast or your local park. Enjoy the warm breeze on your face and feel it invigorate you.

When you rest, you catch your breath and it holds you up, like water wings.

ANNE LAMOTT

••• 05 •••

Sip on iced tea. It's the perfect summertime equivalent to that warm, cosy glass of green tea. It'll cool you off, calm you down and keep you hydrated. Add a sunhat, a lounge chair and a sunny spot if you can spare the time.

••• •••

Hit the beach. Whether that's a lake, ocean or river beach doesn't matter. Just relax in the sun, listen to the water and sink your feet deep into the sand or pebbles. Let the current pull your worries away.

••• (07) •••

Enjoy some childhood joy and peace. Run through a sprinkler in the grass in your bare feet until you forget about anything that's bothering you.

••• (08) •••

Make an effort to wake up early so you have a bit more time in the day and feel less hurried and rushed.

09

Have a nice backyard fire. Invite friends if you want, or keep it quiet and solitary. Take slips of paper and write down your worries, fears, anxieties, grudges and things holding you back. Set the papers in the fire and watch those negative things turn into cleansing fire and freeing ash.

10

Rewatch episodes of your favourite, comforting TV shows. Anything that makes you entirely happy and at ease is the perfect choice.

• • • **11** • • •

Roll a tennis ball, or any other suitable ball, beneath your feet. Press into the ball with your arches, using it as a form of acupressure and stress relief.

12

I am my own experiment.
I am my own work of art.

MADONNA

Grab a newspaper or head online and do a crossword puzzle. While this may perhaps seem stressful in theory, the reality is that focusing your mind on something inconsequential (getting something wrong has no negative effect on you!) pulls you away from the day's stress and quiets the anxious thought patterns. If you really do hate crosswords, though, sudoku or word searches have the same calming effect.

•••(14)•••

I restore myself when I'm alone.

MARILYN MONROE

•••(15)•••

When choosing your morning or evening cup of tea, choose a blend that emphasizes one or more of these herbs and plants, each thought to have a soothing or calming effect: chamomile; passionflower; lavender; catnip; peppermint; gotu kola; rose; ashwagandha; ginseng.

•••(16)•••

Make time to be alone. Constant engagement with others can lead to burnout, but a bit of time set aside to spend entirely by yourself, on your own pursuits, can make a major impact.

Do some mindful, rejuvenating sighing. Yes, that "dramatic" sigh is actually effective at calming you down. When you do deep, conscious breathing, breathe out with an audible, released sigh. Repeat a few times for a nice refocus.

•••(23)•••

Give yourself a tight hug. Wrap your arms around yourself and squeeze tightly, sending love and peace to yourself as well as dispersing tension from the body.

•••(24)•••

Replace dead batteries. That means anywhere around your house where that clock or device has gone dead and you've been neglecting to find new batteries and replace them... just do it now! You'll feel a great little sense of satisfaction and relief.

··• •··

Head outside, sit down and run your fingers through the grass. Sink into it and feel the natural growth beneath you and the soft organic texture of the grass against your fingers.

··• •··

When you recover or discover something that nourishes your soul and brings joy, care enough about yourself to make room for it in your life.

JEAN SHINODA BOLEN

Text your closest friends asking: "What songs always calm you down?" If you have a calm-down playlist in the works, add these. Either way, play them throughout your day when you need a bit of chill time.

••• 28 •••

Tuck into some ice cream, right out of the carton. Don't let yourself feel bad about it for a moment. You deserve a calming, cooling, happy treat.

••• 29 •••

Take a break when you need it, pick up a book, and read to your heart's content. Especially if you read something that's happily escapist, there are few better ways to relax your mind.

30

**Keep good company, read
good books, love good things,
and cultivate soul and body
as faithfully as you can.**

LOUISA MAY ALCOTT

Have you been putting off that computer or phone
restart that keeps popping up? Get it done today,
and you'll have better functioning devices and a
calmer mind by bedtime.

august

Set a new positive, calming mantra for the week and use it every morning. If you can't think of one, try: "I fill my mind and body with peace."

Toss all the hand towels, throw blankets and other often-used fabrics around your house into the laundry. These tend to get neglected on laundry day and could probably do with freshening up. Plus, they'll smell and feel lovely afterward.

Try out a new exercise class or video. Barre, Pilates, spin, kickboxing, or dance!

Start the morning with 10 minutes of slow, methodical stretching. Try some of these options:

- Cobra stretch
- Knee to chest
- Neck stretches
- Side stretch
- Quad stretch

Remember that people don't think as negatively about you as you may assume. In fact, people are probably paying less attention to your tiny mistakes, your music tastes, your outfits and anything else than you think. Most of the negative thoughts you assume others are having about you are actually coming straight from yourself.

••• (06) •••

Try a quick wall push. Plant your feet on the floor near a wall and push firmly against the wall for 5 to 10 seconds, using the movement as a tool to ground you to your space.

••• (07) •••

Find a park with a pond or other water feature where you can watch ducks and swans (and maybe even feed them!).

••• (08) •••

Try some tai chi! This ancient Chinese art involves slow, rhythmic movements and deep breathing, all designed to relieve stress and anxiety, improve your body's functions and even help you get better sleep. The overall result after a short session is a substantially calmer mind and body. You can head to a class or even find instructional videos online.

09

Self-care is the non-negotiable. That's the thing that you have to do.

JONATHAN VAN NESS

10

Hit the beach and go on a leisurely stroll to search for shells, stones and even sea glass. Meander among tide pools or incoming waves and enjoy the simple, calming treasure hunt that a day on the sand can provide.

11

Enjoy some infused water. Add fresh fruit or herbs to your ice water for some extra flavour, refreshment, and to make it more enticing to stay hydrated. Lemons, oranges, apple slices, mint, lavender, rosemary, cucumber and many other tasty treats make great additions.

••• •••

If the day is too much, end it with some calming self-care. Pick a favourite childhood movie, a couple of snacks and grab a nice glass of water. Sink into the comfort that comes from rewatching something you know and love.

••• (13) •••

Invite over the friend you're so comfortable around you don't even need to talk. Do anything that makes you both feel peaceful, whether that's venting about the week, or simply quietly enjoying each other's company.

• • • (14) • • •

Stash a few hard candies in your purse, car, desk or anywhere else you tend to end up feeling uneasy. Suck on one, until it's fully gone, when you need a distracting, calming strategy while engaging in everyday life.

• • • (15) • • •

Have a pajama day. Or better yet, a pajama party. Thrive in comfort and calm.

• • • (16) • • •

Let yourself daydream when you want to. Drifting off into your own imagination is a healthy, normal thing to do and can provide a few moments of calming reprieve from busy life.

17

Every small positive change we
make in ourselves repays us
in confidence in the future.

ALICE WALKER

Get out and take a long, peaceful drive. Head
outside of the city if that's where you live. Try
to take in some greenery or scenery. Pop on your
favourite playlist, put the windows down and truly
enjoy being on the move and in the world, until you
feel calmed down from whatever life is throwing
at you.

••• (19) •••

Cry, if you need to. Holding emotions back or inside is never going to let you feel at peace. When things are making you feel broken, let it out and cry. If life is making you mad, clench your fists and yell out your frustrations. You'll feel calmer after releasing the emotion than if you keep it inside.

••• (20) •••

Fill a big bowl with cold water and ice cubes. Take a deep breath and submerge your entire face, holding it there for about 10 seconds. Feel your body and mind reset – it'll work almost instantly.

••• (21) •••

Wash your dishes right after you use them today.

●●● ●●●
22

Shake it all off. Yes, really. Spend 10-30 seconds shaking your body, top to bottom, and enjoying the mental release that follows.

●●● ●●●
23

Brush or comb your hair. Be slow and gentle to get out any knots, and do it for as long as you can. The improvised head massage provides an instant calming effect, not to mention your hair will look lovely after.

●●● ●●●
24

The most valuable thing we can do for the psyche, occasionally, is to let it rest, wander, live in the changing light of a room.

MAY SARTON

••• •••

Plant some butterfly-attracting plants outside. Keep an eye out for gentle, peaceful visitors as they stop by and delight you.

••• (26) •••

Sit outside to watch the sunset. If you don't have an easy view from your house, head to a park or hill where you can sit and watch the day slowly drift into night.

••• (27) •••

Try some aromatherapy. The easiest and most classic starting point is to pick up a diffuser (there are plenty of sizes and budgets!) and one or two essential oils. Lavender is most known for calming properties. Diffuse the oil throughout the day, particularly in the room where you're most likely to lose your calm.

28

**Activity and rest are two vital
aspects of life. To find a balance
in them is a skill in itself.**

SRI SRI RAVI SHANKAR

29

Grab a hard candy, lollipop or even a candy cane
and suck on it in times of stress. Sometimes a
little sugar kick isn't a bad thing, plus the act
of sucking on something has a great distracting,
soothing effect.

Start the day by journaling about one or more of these questions. See where the answers lead you, and reflect on how you can use this information to build more calming mechanisms into your day and life.

- What is on my mind most this morning?
- What sticks in my mind as I'm falling asleep these days?
- When do I feel most stressed during the day?

Try something unique to get some of your frustrations out. There are all sorts of options out there, from axe throwing to paintballing or even destruction rooms. Specifically designed for you to let off some steam, it'll leave you feeling so much calmer.

september

Tell someone how you really feel. If that means confessing feelings to someone, being honest about a disagreement, or telling your boss you need more support, so be it. Get it off your chest and let yourself feel light.

Enjoy dining al fresco. Sometimes there's a great deal of comfort in a picnic-style meal, whether enjoyed in your own company or with people you love. The sensory combination of the breeze and sun on your skin, the sounds of birds in the trees or people walking by, and the smells of flowers or fresh air can all add a great relaxing effect to a simple meal.

03

I want to feel my life while I'm in it.

MERYL STREEP

Head to some water of any sort and try skipping stones. Choose smooth, pleasant-to-the-touch stones, and spend time throwing each out onto the water and watching for the bounce upon the surface.

05

Go somewhere designed for peace and quiet. A library, museum, botanical garden, or art gallery are all great options. Spend your time there doing anything that calms you personally, and enjoy the tranquil atmosphere the space provides.

Look for repetitive activities to soothe your mind. What works for one person may not for another, so try anything from knitting and crocheting, to chewing gum, petting an animal, jumping rope, or washing dishes, to see what makes you tick.

Seek out some fidget devices, or create your own. Something as simple as a ring that you can wear and spin or stroke in times of worry can provide plenty of relief. However, there are also endless fidgeting-specific tools, gadgets and toys you can purchase and try out, all designed to relieve anxiety and calm the mind.

If you have a dog, you have a calming tool at your disposal every day. Try playing fetch and enjoy the simple joy of your dog returning the ball to you again and again. See how happy they are with simple games, and reflect on simple things that can make you just as happy.

Meditation and praying change your spirit into something positive. If it is already positive, it makes it better.

TINA TURNER

Try a 5-minute guided meditation to start and end your day today.

Add a trickling, bubbling water feature to your home, whether indoors or on a patio or balcony. Pick a spot where you'll be able to enjoy its soothing, calming sounds every day, if you can. There are a huge range of options out there to choose from, whether you want a tiny desktop fountain or a larger statement one for your garden.

••• 12 •••

Where is most of your energy going these days? Reflect on the answer, and whether this is a productive, positive use for your energy or one that is ultimately draining and stressing you.

••• 13 •••

Try a caffeine-free day (or week) and see how your mind and body adjust.

••• (14) •••

If you have a garden, a bird bath is a great addition to calm the mind. While they're available to buy in shops, you can always construct your own bird bath out of any shallow dish adhered to a base. Either way, keep it filled with fresh water and enjoy the pure delight of watching sweet birds pop by for a rinse.

15

In the midst of movement and chaos, keep stillness inside of you.

DEEPAK CHOPRA

Even if you never have, give fishing a try. Known as one of the most calming hobbies in the world, there's a reason so many people love sitting out on a dock or in a boat for hours enjoying the sights and sounds, as well as the methodical tasks of fishing.

Make your cup of tea, but add some lavender, mint, or fresh honey to the cup, any of which will boost the flavour and give you an added calming benefit.

•••(18)•••

Journal each day this week about the things that have been bringing you joy. Small or large, make note of them.

Hang a piece of art or a beloved photo on your wall. Especially if it was blank before, adding a calming, beautiful image to your space will give you a positive boost every time you catch a glimpse of it.

Everybody should just stay at home and meditate and they'd be so much happier.

GEORGE HARRISON

•••（21）•••

Call someone you trust most in the world. If it helps to share your stresses and worries so they're off your chest and you get some support, do so. If it's more helpful to find a bit of distraction in hearing about their day or talking about something unrelated, do that instead!

••• •••

Turn your lavender essential oil into more than a diffusing tool. Add it to a plain lotion to use throughout the day, put a few drops on a piece of fabric and place it under your pillow, or add some to a bath. If lavender scent doesn't calm you, do the same thing with one that does.

••• (23) •••

Recite these affirmations throughout your day:

- I am comfortable with the emotions that flow through me.
- I am calm and relaxed in all that I do.
- Outside influences don't control me.

Flip through photo albums or a slideshow of photos of trips, happy memories, or people you love.

Hit the driving range. You don't need to have ever picked up a golf club in your life to enjoy taking out any negative feelings with some forceful smacking. The point isn't to be good, just to release stress and leave you more calm.

Figure out what actually works for you as calming techniques act differently for different people. Experiment, try some of the following methods and then reuse the ones that really help.

27

Why worry? If you've done the very best you can, worrying won't make it any better.

WALT DISNEY

Sing in the shower. Sing in the car. Sing like you don't care who might hear and how you sound. Just let it out.

Try some emotional freedom technique (EFT) tapping. Like acupuncture or acupressure, but easier to do on your own, this art uses targeted tapping on specific parts of the body to relieve feelings of anxiety. There are lots of ways to do this, and you can always see a practitioner, but you can also find your own techniques that help you out and can be done any time at home. Check out some videos online to get started.

••• 30 •••

Start a jigsaw puzzle. The perfect activity to combine mental distraction and repetitive hand movements, puzzles can take up lots of your time, relax your mind and body, and provide a great sense of accomplishment when you finish one.

october

01

Head to a store that always makes you feel more at ease and relaxed. For some it'll be the packed-to-the-brim bookstore with tucked away armchairs. For others it'll be the plant store filled up with greenery, or an antique store loaded with treasures to admire. Whatever setting you prefer, take yourself there and fully enjoy it.

02

If you're able to enjoy something, to devote your life to it or a reasonable amount of time and energy, it will work out for you.

JERRY GARCIA

••• (03) •••

Take slow, deep breaths, focusing on feeling the air enter and exit from your belly. Picture yourself filling like a balloon as you pull air deeper into your body, letting your stomach inflate as you do. Belly breathing is a more wholesome, soothing way of moving air through your body consciously.

••• (04) •••

Ask someone special to you (a grandparent, parent, or best friend, for example) if they have any small jewellery items or a blanket they could pass on to you. Let them know you'll keep it close by to remind you of them and calm you down in times of stress.

••• (05) •••

If you work from home, changing locations and scenery can help your mind reset. Cafés and libraries make for much more peaceful workspaces.

Try doing a popular yoga position called downward-facing dog. Press your heels toward the floor, raise your hips up high, and feel the stretch throughout the muscles of your body. Hold this position for a minute or so, flexing your legs to get more stretch.

●●● 07 ●●●

Get a first aid kit in order. If you know you'll be more prepared for an injury or accident, you can let go of a bit of anxiety. So, make sure your house, car and maybe even purse each have a first aid kit. Include bandages, antibiotic creams, wraps, medications, ice packs and anything else you think you might need.

· · ● (08) ● · ·

Reread your favourite book. Or just parts of it, if you know it well enough to slide in and out of the story with ease.

· · ● (09) ● · ·

Start using natural room sprays with fresh, calming scents. Brighten the aroma of your space while simultaneously aromatically calming yourself. You could even make a homemade one.

· · ● (10) ● · ·

Keep a rocking chair in your home or outdoor space. Sit here in moments of worry and rock yourself gently into a calmer headspace.

Try some kickboxing. If you go to a gym, you can use their punching bags, or you could always get one for your house if you think it might be helpful. Release stress, anxiety, tension and worry with each thrust of your arms or legs. In return, breathe in peace and contentment.

Rest more intentionally. When you're taking "relaxing time" don't actually spend it checking social media and emails, catching up on chores, or worrying about work. Make rest time sacred and truly for rest, and all of those things can have their own separate times.

Put together a calming toolbox. This should be a basket that collects any fidget tools you like to use. They may be ones you've purchased, or household items whose tactile sensations provide a distracting and calming effect. Consider: silly putty, hair ties, rings or jewellery to fiddle with, smooth stones, a ball to roll under your feet, a clothespin to open and close, a lavender sachet, or anything else that helps.

Make your own soothing, gentle oatmeal face mask. Cook a serving of oatmeal and mix with two tablespoons of honey. Once cool, apply to your face and let sit for about 10 minutes before rinsing off.

15

I am my own sanctuary.

LADY GAGA

If you find yourself in the midst of a drizzly, damp day, head outside for a little stroll. Let yourself get a bit wet, and enjoy taking in the lovely smells and sounds of falling rain. Toss on some boots and a raincoat if you have them, and you can even jump in some puddles!

Find a hammock to laze away an afternoon in. A worthwhile investment for anyone who wants to be more calm, hammocks are a thoroughly lovely spot to rock slowly in the breeze, enjoy the sun and birdsong, and even take a nap. If any seating option can be considered a relaxation haven, hammocks may top the list.

Get out some paper and colouring materials and draw. There is no pressure to be "good" or make something to display – it's just for you. Doodle, scribble, colour, trace. Try whichever technique is most therapeutic to you.

• • • (19) • • •

Listen to an audiobook or podcast when you need a little auditory stimulation to distract or amuse you.

●●● ●●●

If you can, travel by train. Rather than getting stuck in traffic and ramping up your own tension, drift into a state of relaxation with the steady motion of the wheels on the tracks. It takes away all the need to focus, getting frustrated by bad drivers, or worry about routes. Just hop on and hop off, and enjoy your trip more.

●●● 21 ●●●

Bake something! Even if you don't make it from scratch and opt to use a mix (no shame there!), filling your home with the smell of delicious treats throughout the day is delightful and purely soothing to the mind.

Make a flower or succulent arrangement for your home. Buying a bouquet has its pleasures, but taking flowers you purchase or collect and arranging them in a complex, beautiful display for your table makes it into an entire, calming activity. If you aren't as much for flowers, you can also take a long, wide planter and make an adorable succulent arrangement.

• • • (23) • • •

To start your morning, make a huge smoothie loaded up with fruits, vegetables and anything else you love.

• • • (24) • • •

Write a poem. You don't need to have any traditional skill or experience to do so. Just take out a notebook and turn your feelings – good or bad – into something more beautiful.

••• (25) •••

Sometimes you'll have some things, and sometimes you'll have other things. And you do not need it all at once; it's not good for you.

EMMA THOMPSON

••• (26) •••

Use a slow cooker. Add some simple ingredients to it in the morning, turn it on and head off on your day. In one quick step you've completely eliminated any stress about what you'll eat for dinner, or the work it'll take to cook when you get home. Instead, delicious warm food will be waiting to calm you after your day.

••• (27) •••

Look after a caterpillar until it turns into a butterfly. There are kits that help you do this and include the supplies you need. Watching this tiny creature go through its life cycle – from caterpillar to cocoon to butterfly – in front of you provides a beautiful, soothing distraction.

••• (28) •••

Smile at people you pass by. Not only will you have the knowledge that you're spreading some positivity, but you might also get some encouraging smiles in return, and be reminded that there is plenty of good around you.

••• (29) •••

Head online and watch cute animal videos until you can't help feeling better.

Set a pot of water on the stove and add delicious, aromatic elements such as orange and lemon peels, cinnamon sticks, whole nutmegs and cloves, and so on. Heat the water for as long as you like, and let the sweet fragrance waft through the house.

Write a story. Again, it's never about being traditionally "good" at an artistic pursuit, but about letting your mind take a break from the worries and chaos getting to you. Simply focus on creativity and escapism. Write a picture book, a fantasy tale, a bit of romance, or anything else you please.

november

Find a real-life "happy place" near your home where you can repeatedly go. Choose a favourite café, bar, park, store, or anywhere else that immediately makes you feel good and safe when you walk in. Think of this intentionally as your calm spot. Return each time you need to calm down, leaving only once you feel more at peace. Over time your brain will associate this place with calm more quickly.

It's easier to be brave when you're not alone.

AMY POEHLER

Meditate, and add some extra elements. Try it near moving water or rain. Add a guided voice or tranquil music. Diffuse essential oils nearby, or try a comfy new cushion to sit on.

• • • (04) • • •

Make something delicious from scratch that you normally wouldn't. Pop popcorn on the stove and season it yourself, rather than using the microwave. Or brew a massive pitcher of iced tea for your fridge. Try making your own spice blends, or hot sauce, or salsa. Get into the process and let it distract you.

Try "earthing". Sometimes also called grounding, this popular practice of going barefoot has a powerful soothing effect. In your own garden or a park you love, kick off your shoes and feel at one with nature as you connect to the ground beneath you.

Learning how to be still, to really be still and let life happen – that stillness can become a radiance.

MORGAN FREEMAN

••• 07 •••

Clean a room of your house, from top to bottom. Get it sparkling, so it's a fully soothing, worry-free place to spend time in.

Head online and search for live feeds from animal sanctuaries, petting zoos, or similar places. Many set up 24/7 cams so you can tune in anytime you need to chill out and watch some baby animals playing or napping.

Try some white noise. You can pick up a machine, or just play sounds online. Things like rainfall, lapping waves, crickets whirring, or birdsong can all be lovely background sounds to your work or even sleep.

Try to start and complete tasks well ahead of their deadline, so when the deadline does roll around you have no worries about it and can focus on other things.

Try lighting incense. While this isn't for everyone, there are a variety of scents designed to calm and refresh you. In particular, lemongrass, jasmine, sandalwood or chamomile incense are great at helping you unwind.

Check out autonomous sensory meridian response (ASMR) videos online. In these videos, creators will use their voices or a range of materials to make gentle, quiet sounds that can be very soothing to the mind. The range of options is huge, so there's likely to be something that strikes a pleasing chord in your brain. Studies show more and more that ASMR really does calm us down, so why not give it a try?

13

**The quieter you become,
the more you can hear.**

RAM DASS

••• **14** •••

Schedule pockets of designated, intentional rest
and relaxation time throughout the week. This will
help calm enter your life more frequently and lets
you look forward to these moments too.

••• **15** •••

Go through your junk drawer (we all have one) and
clear out what you don't need. Tidy up, organize it
a bit, and leave it in better shape.

Do something kind for someone. Taking your focus off yourself for a bit, to expend some energy and attention on someone else, can feel greatly rewarding, and is a soothing distraction from your worries.

Make your own fancy, infused oils. It's simple and satisfying. Just fill up a glass jar or bottle with olive oil and add any ingredients you want. This could be hot chillies, fresh garlic, basil, rosemary, lemon or orange peels, or just about anything else you dream up.

••• 18 •••

Thoroughly clean your shoes or nicest jewellery. Dedicate an hour to methodically cleaning some well-loved items that rarely get cleaned and end up with a beautiful, satisfying result.

19

When I started counting my blessings, my whole life turned around.

WILLIE NELSON

Make a homemade bubble bath. Simply mix about 59 g (¼ cup) of warm water, 118 g (½ cup) of your favourite liquid soap, and 59 g (¼ cup) of coconut oil. You could also add a couple of drops of skin-safe essential oil. Add it to a hot bath and enjoy.

••• (21) •••

Buy or make a weighted blanket. In times of
anxiety, curl up under it and feel the weight
pressing down like a comforting, calming hug.

••• (22) •••

If you tend to be cold, use a heating pad on your
legs, stomach or lower back to radiate soothing
warmth throughout your body.

••• (23) •••

Give yourself a manicure or pedicure. Painting
is optional, but you can soak your hands or feet
in warm, soapy water, do a little hand or foot
massage, rub lotion in, clip your nails and cuticles,
and generally take care of these hard-worked
parts of your body.

When anxiety runs amok, sit and stare at a fixed object – a tree, chair, window, picture or lamp, for example – and repeat again and again in your head the name of what you're looking at. Let your thoughts be entirely consumed by the sight of this object and its name on a loop in your head. You won't be able to focus on any of the things that were causing your original anxiety.

Keep a good heart. That's the most important thing in life.

JONI MITCHELL

Jump up and down. On a trampoline, if it's an option, using a skipping rope, or for no reason at all other than to clear away fog in your brain and let the peace in.

Grab a canvas or poster board, some paints, and splatter it. Don't bother with brushes or technique, just let loose and splash, smear and rub the paint, using your hands and letting yourself be messy.

••• 28 •••

Fix something in your house that's broken and you've been putting off for no reason. Simple satisfying tasks like replacing a button on a favourite shirt can get put off for months, but take no more than a few moments to finish up.

Travel for the sole purpose of self-care, rejuvenation and relaxation. This can fit any budget, from a lavish beach trip to a simple weekend away from home in a cottage with no phone service and plenty of cosy things to wrap up in.

Challenge your yoga skills. Try hot yoga (in a heated room), acroyoga (adding in aerial movements or acrobatics), or do yoga moves on a stand-up paddle board on water if you're particularly well-balanced!

december

Respond to all the lingering, unopened or flagged emails in your inbox. Clear out the clutter and you'll clear away some of your stresses in the meantime.

Worry never robs tomorrow of its sorrow, it only saps today of its joy.

LEO BUSCAGLIA

••• •••

Choose a throw blanket that brings you the most comfort, whether it was gifted or made by someone you love, it's particularly soft, or it holds a positive memory. Leave it on your lap throughout the day. Let its presence and feel in your hands bring calm.

••• (04) •••

Think back to a year or two ago. Day-to-day, what were you worrying about? Do you remember? This can be a good reminder that the fears and worries that plague us are often temporary, and worth much less of our energy.

••• (05) •••

Back up your phone and computer storage so you can rest assured you won't lose anything important.

••• 06 •••

Take a moment to close your eyes, take a deep breath and visualize yourself sitting next to the ocean. You're soaked in warm, comfortable sun and have a cold drink in your hand. You're lounging on a soft chair and have an umbrella keeping the sun out of your eyes. You have nothing to do and are simply listening to the waves move back and forth.

07

That the birds of worry and care fly over your head, this you cannot change, but that they build nests in your hair, this you can prevent.

CHINESE PROVERB

Grab any face mask, whether homemade or store bought. You may already have a favourite. A now-cliché tool of self-care, perhaps, but no less beneficial for caring for both your skin and your mind at once. Relax your facial muscles while you use it.

••• 09 •••

Channel your inner child. You can probably remember how much more relaxed and at ease you felt when you were a kid — or that the worries you did have were actually small things. Find joy in the small beauties and joys now. Make an effort to be delighted by simple wonders.

Avoid putting off or holding onto things. The longer you do, the more space it takes up in your mind. And the less room you have for peace.

Drive around your hometown or an area you felt happy as a child. Drive past childhood homes, schools or parks where you'd play as a kid. Revel in the good memories of times when you were younger and had fewer cares.

••• 12 •••

Look around online for some mindfulness videos. There are a whole range out there, from therapists giving step-by-step tricks for being calmer, to mindfulness mantras and meditations. Pick one and follow along when you need a little outside support.

**Keep smiling, because life is
a beautiful thing and there's
so much to smile about.**

MARILYN MONROE

If you feel totally overwhelmed, call someone or
go visit them, and tell them how you're feeling.
Don't underplay your emotions; freely and openly
let them know about your worries, fears, and
struggles (as long as they're in the headspace for
it!). Speaking things out loud releases them from
their prison in your head, and lets you get space
from them, freeing you to feel a bit more calm.

••• (**15**) •••

Create a ritual. Small daily rituals can be highly
therapeutic and help you feel much more relaxed
going into work or about your daily tasks. Your
ritual could be anything, or a combination of
things. Stretching, reciting mantras, meditating,
listening to music, hot or cold showers – the
options are endless. The key is routine.

••• (**16**) •••

Visit YouTube and watch some aerial exploration
videos. Perhaps not ideal for those very prone
to motion sickness, but otherwise amazing for
providing a soothing sense of calm and wonder,
these videos make you feel like you're flying over
beautiful landscapes.

••• (**17**) •••

Take three massive, deep breaths in through your
noise and out (loudly) through your mouth.

I will be calm. I will be mistress of myself.

JANE AUSTEN

••• 19 •••

Forgive yourself. More important than almost anything is being kind and gentle with yourself. Rather than beating yourself up about small mistakes or fears, be endlessly forgiving, and simply strive to learn and improve next time.

••• 20 •••

Watch some videos and learn to crochet. Then pull out your crochet project each time you need a calming, repetitive task to soothe your soul.

Make a list of the hardest things you've dealt with in your life. Read through it. You survived each of these things. Remember that fact, and that the things you're handling now will someday be like the ones on your list – in the past, far behind you.

•• ● (22) ● ••

Sit in front of a window where you can watch animals, or head to a big open field. Be peaceful and still and simply exist in the moment, waiting to see what will appear, whether birds, squirrels, rabbits, deer, or someone else entirely.

•• ● (23) ● ••

Drink a glass of ice-cold water, slowly, sip by sip. Don't rush; instead enjoy each glug.

Clean your bathroom. Do your most thorough job, getting to every corner and nook, even dusting your décor, cleaning the glass and restocking things like toilet paper and soap.

••• 25 •••

Make a warm drink and share it with loved ones. Hot chocolate, eggnog, coffee, tea or mulled cider all make great choices.

••• 26 •••

Carefully fill your living space with candles and light them, one by one. Turn off other lights, and enjoy the flickering, serene lighting all around you.

27

In the madness,
you have to find calm.

LUPITA NYONG'O

••• •••

Relieve yourself of admin worries by creating one secure location for all of your most important documents, photos and things like lists of medications, insurance, important phone numbers, and so on. If you can, put these things into a binder, sealed in a plastic bag, and you'll be ready for anything.

Take a nap. Set an alarm for when you need to be up again, make the room cosy and then let yourself drift off for a while.

••• (30) •••

Treat yourself to a day at the spa. Whether it's for a facial, massage, soak, or any other treatment, you deserve some high-end relaxation and pampering now and again.

••• (31) •••

If pondering New Year's resolutions causes you nothing but anxiety and feelings of pressure, skip them this year. Instead try an alternative, like making a simple list of fun things you want to do during the year, or creating a list of affirmations or mantras that can guide you throughout the seasons to come.

conclusion

If this book proves anything, I hope it's that there is no one right way to bring more calm into your mind, body and world. In fact, what works for each person will differ entirely, so by trying out the ideas in this book, you'll be able to create a wonderfully calming toolkit of the ones that are best suited for you.

Each of us, as we go through life, experiences a huge range of emotions, even on a daily basis. It's a part of being human and living in a fast-moving, imperfect world. But knowing that peace, calm and tranquillity are only ever a moment or a simple action away makes all of the hard parts and worries a little easier to handle.

also available

365 DAYS OF INSPIRATION

ISBN: 978-1-80007-444-6

Robyn Martin

365 DAYS OF MINDFUL MEDITATIONS

ISBN: 978-1-80007-101-8

Karen Edwards

365 DAYS OF POSITIVITY

ISBN: 978-1-80007-102-5

Debbi Marco

365 DAYS OF KINDNESS

ISBN: 978-1-80007-100-1

Vicki Vrint

365 DAYS OF YOGA

ISBN: 978-1-78783-641-9

Have you enjoyed this book?
If so, find us on Facebook at
Summersdale Publishers, on Twitter
at @Summersdale and on Instagram
at @summersdalebooks and get in
touch. We'd love to hear from you!

www.summersdale.com